"Throughout this triumphant collection, Dani Putney stretches again and again across the Pacific, searching for some way to be 'the most Filipinx version / of myself' — a 'yearning for an archipelago / denied to me at conception' that juxtaposes uneasily, in fact brilliantly, with the yearning of American men for Filipina women. Caught between two countries and three languages, *Mix-Mix* will suspend you, too, in the traditional Filipino dessert [Halo-Halo] of which [Mix-Mix] is the English translation: you'll find yourself in a tall glass, surrounded by the sweet, the colorful, and the cold."

— Kimberly Quiogue Andrews, *A Brief History of Fruit*

"Dani Putney's second full-length collection, *Mix-Mix*, is sharp and smart and vulnerable. The poems move across time and space as the speaker explores and interrogates identity, sexuality, family history, and intergenerational trauma. The speaker writes: 'Imagination is all I have / when history gives me nothing. Percent / this, percent that, but my blood burns / for a vigil full of ghosts. I want to know / who I am, but I only find my father's / grave. Am I already dead?' Indeed, imagination buoys the reader alongside the speaker through the haunting guides to 'marriage by correspondence,' the dissection of gender theory, and finally, the journey to understand the self and find a place to come home to."

— Roseanna Alice Boswell, *Hiding in a Thimble*

"Yes, imagination is potentiality and nourishment, and the future is malleable, yielding under the brown body's efforts to find home in both self and surroundings. Putney's important collection proclaims 'I am the ultimate possibility' — an anthem for the colonized everywhere."

— Ina Cariño, *Feast*

"Dani Putney's *Mix-Mix* delivers on its unforgettable namesake — a treasured Filipinx dessert made of shaved ice, milk, and a myriad of ingredients that guarantee no serving will be the same. It is as textured, complex, and astonishing in its explorations and articulations of the self as sprouted from America's troubling history of correspondence marriages. Every poem is savored newly on the palate. What a packed collection this is from a truly invigorating poet."

— Janine Joseph, *Decade of the Brain*

"The title of this book, *Mix-Mix*, is the English translation of the Filipino dessert halo-halo. Halo-halo is a layered dessert, made up of beans and fruit and topped with shaved ice, condensed milk, ice cream, and leche flan in a clear glass. Similar to this dessert, *Mix-Mix* examines the layers of yearnings, confusions, and loves within the speaker's hybrid history and intersectional identity. It asks: How did we travel from here to here? How were we deprived by and lured toward America, toward its hollow calories, which leave us 'forever gutom,' forever underfed? These poems offer a kind of antidote to imperial deprivation. As soon as I opened this book, I felt that I was being invited to a family member's home, that I was being offered a meal, that I was being told the truth. Dani Putney's *Mix-Mix* is a beautiful and profoundly satisfying read, shaped by this speaker's vulnerability, empathy, and artistic brilliance."

— Marianne Chan, *All Heathens*

"In *Mix-Mix*, the reader may feel the inescapable weight of Putney's circumstances stemming from the life one is born into. This is only in order for Putney to better illustrate how empowering those personal truths can become if given the chance and how illuminating those same truths can prove to be in helping us find our place in the world. *Mix-Mix*, as a testament to such self-discovery, will resonate long after the final page has been turned and culminates in a stirring collection of poems that burn and crackle in the light of unwavering faith in the fact that a life truly lived must be fully examined, no matter the cost."

— T.K. Lee, *Scapegoat*

mix-mix

MIX-MIX

poems

Dani Putney

First American Edition

ISBN-13: 978-1-936097-56-2

Library of Congress Control Number: 2024950313

Baobab Press
316 California Ave, #24
Reno, Nevada 89509
www.baobabpress.com

for my mom,

always

Contents

Miscegenation

Heritage

Dad was born in 1939.
I was born in 1996.
4 of my 7 siblings were born
before you, Ma. Did you visit
Pampanga as a kid?
That's where your step-
children were raised.

3 wives, 57 years, & 7,000
miles away from your Talisay
home only makes sense
if I say *colonialism*, Ma.
Time & distance must be
products of your zeitgeist,
a suspension in *post* —

why did you & Dad
make me in America?
Ma, I can call you *nanay*
in 3 languages except my own.
I have no birthright.
My unborn body lost its roots
in 1957 after Dad graduated

from his segregated
high school — Falls Church,
Virginia — & the Air Force
assigned him to Clark AB.
Ma, his Oriental desire
was set, & I lost, years before
1991, when you were 24

❦

& he took you to California.
I want to know him, & you,
but I only have numbers.
Tell me, Ma, how you live
separated from your culture.
You say I'm lucky to be here,
but I think you're wrong:

Luck is not being born at all.

Asian Romance Guide to Marriage by Correspondence

July 8, 1989

Dear Jasmin,

Greetings from the Golden
State of California   your photo
& brief description compelled me
to write

I am [American Man], 36
years old, 5 ft. 10 inches, 145
pounds   a dentist, I have a small
practice   during days off I tend
my variety of fruit   apple, peach,
cherry, plum   I enjoy canning
& making pies   my peaches
are ripening

Jasmin, I am serious
about finding a Filipina wife,
heaven knows I could use help
around the house   I am interested
to hear about your nursing course
& what you admire about me

In my next letter, I promise
to answer your questions   thanks
for your time   young lady   I hope
to have you soon

Respectfully,
Sam

PS: Send a photo of your [fruit],
it would be so kind

Dear Darren Criss

It's a shame you're straight,
as in I imagined myself snuggled
in Blaine's — no, *your* — Dalton Academy
blazer post-coitus. I would've known you
better than Kurt, than yourself. Aren't

we the same, a mixed-yellow Californian
with our dead buried in Cebu? I, too,
know San Francisco's Castro District.
I've caressed the fog of your Catholic
childhood: What's more intimate, I ask.

You stole me the moment Katy Perry
flew off your tongue. I awoke inside
your all-boys paradise. There, your voice
warbled into me, vuela por mis pulmones
— no, mi amor, they were always yours.

I yearned for you before I learned to want
myself, this queer little heart. Your gaze,
that's what you left me, a trail of hazel
confetti to lead me back to the crossroads
of our teenage dream. You married

a woman, but I still think of our olive
hands intertwined, two Pinoy mongrels
against them all. I can never forgive you,
as in I refuse to stop falling in love
with us.

Picasso Bleeds

Artists speak of me
with Rodin on their tongues,
chiseling me in the ventricles
of their minds, erecting
a nouveau David to flatter
Michelangelo, coating
my skin with Renaissance
limestone. But my bones
            breathe: melting clocks
        & atmospheric skulls
    feed calcium to my body's
        impression.   I'm lost
  on Duchamp's naked staircase,
    a war along my blue-yellow skin.

Footnotes to Marriage by Correspondence

THE ENGAGEMENT

It is best to prepare your fiancée
for life in America
Drivers' Education: very few ladies
know how to drive   we recommend that
you send your special Filipina to driving
school   consider mailing her a pamphlet
covering motor vehicle laws in the States
College Education: almost always
a waste of time   Philippine universities
grant degrees that are meaningless
in the [West]   it is advisable that you have
the merits of her education evaluated
by a foreign transcript system
Dental Visit: the Immigration
& Naturalization Service requires Filipinas
traveling to the US to undergo a complete
medical exam   one part of this is a dental
[appraisal]   several shiny new fillings
will be a point in your favor   if additional
work is needed, your dentist in America
should take care of it
Immigration: only those who fall
into categories of highest priority will be
allowed in the United States   the fact is
that an unacceptably high percentage
of Filipinos on "tourist" or "student" visas
stay illegally   for your wife to be granted
an entry visa, you must assure INS that you
are capable of supporting your dependent
spouse & that your marriage is most likely
genuine

Footnotes to Marriage by Correspondence

YOUR PHOTOGRAPH

Selecting the right photo to send
with your initial letter is very important,
as Filipinas are more attracted to clean-
shaven men than those sporting mustaches
or beards
Filipinas are also intimidated
by large men   the ladies you will write
weigh between 90 & 120 pounds   if
you are a little overweight, portray
your lighter side
Look dignified, posing in a suit
& tie   as much as possible, your photo
should convey neatness, respectability,
& [power]

Kumusta

ka, how are you, cómo
te va. I can kiss you in 3
tongues, stranger, let me
know how you want it. Like
a snake, I swallow whole.
I've been called a *global*
citizen, but I prefer *exotic*.
I only sleep with dirty-blond,
blue-eyed boys because I
can't forget I'm special.
I read in a textbook once
that Asian American women
marry white men, whether
deliberately or sub-
consciously, to assimilate.
Lover, I'm thinking of this
sociological "phenomenon"
when I tell you I'm more like
my mother than my father.
I've inherited the girl who
wanted to inhale the New
World. Have I told you I'm
non-binary. Don't worry —
it's not gay if you're fucking
nothing. (My salted skin
tastes of everything.)
So I repeat, sir: what language
do you need me to be in.

Dear Andrew Cunanan

When you smashed
Jeff's head in, the love
of your life's mouth agape
across the living room,
I was there, a fourth
presence in the apartment,
learning from the greatest
sugar-daddy killer in queer
history. Though I was born

a year before in your Cali
home, my soul astral-
projected to that night
in Minneapolis, a day after
my parents' anniversary.
Diwata carried the flame
of my spirit to you for a lesson
in balance: fire doused
in the city of water, a Filipino

embroiled in the intimacy
of white death. I fused
with you then to form a whole
person, your half of Luzon,
mine of Cebu — no need
for David, Lee, or Gianni
in our purgatory of gay
mongrelhood, our torso
clad in gilded Oroton.

Some say you were
a psycho, but I only saw *you*
with my baby eyes: a tempest
unstuck in American empire,
a bundle of entropy
much too premature
for the future we deserve.
In this life we're but tiyanak,
Drew, lost in trails of blood.

Footnotes to Marriage by Correspondence

STATIONERY

Get off to a good start   create
a favorable impression with custom
stationery   you must ensure that
your letter stands out
Many of the ladies you will write
have other pen friends   handwritten
letters get the best response,
& we recommend that you send these
personalized [contracts] to your first
choices   include an impersonal
typewritten letter for the hundreds more
Your envelope will be noticeable
if you use several attractive
commemorative stamps   stickers
depicting cartoon characters or reflective
holograms are always well received
by teenage [girls]

Coordinates for My Dad's Ashes

Apostrophe:
I didn't want to write

for you, for me,
because I might spell

forgiveness, the same feeling —
or is it an action? —

Ma said anchored
your sclerosed heart.

(You can already see
I'm not good at this.)

I needed to believe
you were God:

It's easy to destroy
a monolith, your whiteness,

a penchant for the Orient,
the skinny boy who discovered

Luzon beauties
& never looked back.

Alternatively, I found
psychoanalysis:

There was a blond man
(I think we have the same type)

❦

who gave you a camera & said,
Remember me.

I glimpse your chests painted
with Mid-Atlantic scum,

I want to lick the photograph,
maybe I'll understand why

you denied me this memory
& instead talked about

gay prison rape.
Call me the id

to your ego — it's simple.
I still tell everyone

your conquest was denial,
a route forged in tropical storms

& the sweet taste
of mangoes.

You found an archipelago
while I found men

to replace you.
(Is my honesty

too sentimental?)
But I know I can't

write around your body,
much like I can't

❦

throw away the scrap of paper
where I left you:

Latitude: 39.37
Longitude: –120.12

Philippines

Halo-halo

Tucked in a fluorescent corner
of my go-to mini mart is chicken
adobo, a row of fish heads,
& my mom's favorite, pork
blood stew. After a decade
of visits, the café shines the same:
a couple of *kumustas*, steel ladle
on steel tray, Styrofoam boxes
foolishly compartmentalized.
Maraming salamat po —

but I remind Ma to buy halo-
halo, *Yes, you said you would.*
I see myself in the cup's crushed
ice, scattered like islands
throughout an archipelago,
the shards of my DNA floating
in evaporated milk. Add coconut,
sweetened beans, & gulaman,
& I'm my parents' child:

lighter than the Visayas,
darker than Virginia state.

What if I grew up outside
America, a mestizo transplant?
I wouldn't use whitening lotion
to become a Pinoy model
of the West. My nose would have
the right type of crooked, my chin
the perfect dash of stubble.
Heterogeneous treats
come standard with twice-
colonized island nations.

❦

Like ube, my color would be
undeniable: no doubts
under hot fluorescents, no more
dessert metaphors. My brown feet
would mirror Ma's brown feet,
a bowl of dinuguan between us,
her face just a face,
no longer a reflection
of our homeland.

Asian Romance Guide to Marriage by Correspondence

October 22, 1989

Dear Annabelle,

You may be surprised
to receive this unsolicited letter
from America   I saw a photo
& a brief description   you seem
like my type of lady
I will be honest, I am very
interested in finding a Filipina
lifetime partner   my name is
[American Man], friends call me
Skip   42, divorced, no children,
I work as a forklift operator
for a major oil company in Anchorage
& earn a good living
You may have heard Alaska
is a cold, deserted place   I could
hardly ask for more beauty
or [property]   I surely have no
trouble staying warm in my 3-
bedroom home
A letter from you would be
magnificent   please tell me about
your life goals & describe what you do
in a typical day   I would be
very happy to take time with a recent
photo of yourself

Sincerely,
Skip

Killing Field

In his homily, Fr. Harvey talked about "unsettled souls" or what Cebuanos call "mga kalag nga wa mahiluna" and how his Marian devotion helped him to cope with the spiritual needs of parishioners.
— Malou Guanzon Apalisok, "Honoring the dead,"
Cebu Daily News (October 31, 2016)

Nanay tells me about the dead bodies outside
her Talisay home: the 1970s murder spree
by communist insurgents within the heart
of the Visayas. She speaks matter-of-factly,
as if decay were her birthright, piles of stiff
limbs a girl's typical walk-to-class scenery.

I want to ask her *why*, as if she could explain
slaughter, but I recall my US birth & silently
laugh. I chew on my tongue because I'm stupid
to think there's a *more* to massacre, a rhetoric
to shroud the reflection of Ma's hometown:
a mass graveyard. I imagine, years before,

aswang sniffing out corpses in public school
restrooms & hidden berms, a humanoid sheen
across the ghouls' eyes spelling *hunger*, or *joy*.
As in, battle-born flesh tastes of palabok,
that mix of savory pork & salty shrimp restless
spirits leave behind on skin like a remember-

me, like last week's buried pot of kimchi.
I wish them peace, I lie to her. I hope, in secret,
that the souls were all devoured. Blood seeps
into the afterlife & pollutes it with trauma
that conquers pedigrees. I was born with ghosts
in my eyes: I look at Ma,

yearn to eat hers.

Otap

I know I'm home when I see
striped-green awnings, a cardboard
Pikachu face smiling from the window,
& *Asian Market* written in sans-serif
blocks. The aisle closest to the door
is my favorite: all the goodies to hoard
in my pantry. Boy Bawang corn nuts
to Hello Panda biscuits, Royal Family
mochi to spicy Samyang seaweed.

I remember my first trip to Crepe Myrtle,
a lalaki on a mission. I scanned
the snack section for Cebu's finest
puff pastry. I didn't expect Shamrock —
that's pasalubong fare — but it seemed
like my luck was nonexistent.
After inspecting the rest of the mart,
grabbing extra Nongshim ramen
& too many sachets of jasmine tea,

I decided to peruse the small bites
once more for good measure.
I'll never forget the bag's translucent
plastic & green font: *Product of
the Philippines. Eureka*, the European
in me might have cried,
but I instead whispered *Salamat*.

Footnotes to Marriage by Correspondence

YOUR LETTERS I

The ladies you are writing to have
grown up in a culture vastly different
from that of America   this difference
explains the attractive traits of Filipinas,
but it also makes it difficult to assess how
she will react to life here

Children: average family consists
of six children   families with ten, twelve,
or sixteen not uncommon   even educated
ladies cannot conceive of the importance
their own life will assume in America
with their activities & so on   you will
both laugh when you reflect on her former
plan to have six children

Religion & Philosophy: Catholic
because her parents are Catholic   again,
even intelligent ladies cannot conceive
of choosing their own philosophy of life,
so she believes what every good Catholic
believes   further questions are pointless

Life Insurance & Wills: should be
avoided throughout courtship   even after
you are happily married, Filipinas will find
the purchase of life insurance abhorrently
objectionable   extends to drawing up
a legally binding will   most notably,
Germans have married Filipinas, purchased
large life insurance policies on them, & had
the women murdered

AIDS: if you become engaged & she
asks you to have an AIDS test, this is not
something to be alarmed about   her lesser
[brain] fears that many Americans are
infected

Footnotes to Marriage by Correspondence

YOUR LETTERS II

Sex: not to be avoided entirely, it is
a subject you should treat with discretion,
as many ladies are proudly virgins, & others
would be extremely offended if asked
if they had sexual experience   refrain
from mentioning sex until a serious letter-
writing relationship has developed   virtue
& innocence make Filipinas the best wives
Vasectomy: you are likely to be
misunderstood if you try to express this
in a letter   discuss you have undergone
a [sin] with her in person
Race: few Filipinas have ever met
a Black man   if you are Black, wait until
your fourth letter before sending ladies
a photo   don't despair, some Filipinas do,
indeed, marry Afro-Americans
Vocabulary: English is her second
language   avoid long words & use ordinary
phrases   the extent of her verbal abilities
will become apparent after you receive
several letters   to add spice: Gimahal
ko ang imong litrato

Dela Torre

One sound can mean
the difference between *America*
& *alien*. Linguists describe
this phenomenon as articulation:
tongue moves forward, muscles
contract around the vowel.
Have you ever wondered
what makes an accent seem
foreign? Mouth organs have
different settings, ask any gringo
in Spanish class. I'm set

to American English, a patriot
in my voice. I must remind
phone bankers of another SoCal
Democrat who surfs too much.
I was raised to believe
the immigrant dream meant living
indistinguishably, but if you
pronounce my first name
with an unrounded vowel,
I'll know you understand treason.
Ma left her Philippine tower

so I could call her *mother* in perfect
English, but my lips crave
the saltwater shores of Mactan.
My name feels most real
when it sounds like Lapu-Lapu:
a mango against my cheek.
When I speak Spanish, I think of
my mom's famous sunburn story —
she fell asleep on a beach near

her childhood home. I was born
with Ma's blaze along my tongue,

her plea to never forget our past:
colonization in two languages.

Balikbayan

Every OF knows this. My mom is no exception. We'd head to the closest LBC, Jollibee around the corner. All branches must be located at strip malls. Maybe California is just a strip mall. I don't remember what we'd put in those red boxes. I only know we sent "rich" American money — we paid for my cousin's nursing education. *They think we're all rich*, Ma always tells me. What *we* is that? I think it's funny how my mom wants to be American while I want to be Filipino. She's more *we* than myself, but I can still check *citizen* while she has to renew her green card. In this country you're only permanent until renewal. I joke that postcolonialism is a bigger word for *compromise*. Is that melodrama, or is it a cry for help: *Take a box from my past, tell me I'm enough*. I didn't understand my niece when she asked why I wasn't white because she wasn't either. I hate my mom for thinking I am because I have a US passport. A couple of years ago, the day before Ma turned 52, my cousin, the nurse, Facebook-messaged me: *Dani, your uncle Arturo is dying*. She included a photo of him almost dead. *Please tell your mom*. Ma was upset, *Matet cursed my birthday*. Exactly 52 years after my mom was born, her brother died in their native Cebu. I was part of the family that July afternoon, my heart's rhythm inside the balikbayan box. I have the picture to prove —

Asian Romance Guide to Marriage by Correspondence

October 20, 1989

Dear Carmelita,

What a pleasure it is
to write such a lovely young
lady   her robe a cloud, her face
a flower
My name is [American
Man], I live in a townhouse
on the outskirts of Huntsville,
Alabama   I taught high school
for 26 years, 7 as vice principal   66
years old, I live on a very adequate
retirement pension
I am in excellent physical
shape   I work out 3 times a week,
never smoke, seldom drink,
the real matter of importance is
not a person's age but the love
within his heart
My wife of 35 years died
suddenly, I wish to make a fresh
start   a simple, lighthearted lady
who enjoys adventure   I have
a motor home to travel around
this grand [empire]
I believe in faithfulness,
gentle lady   I look forward
to having your pleasure soon

Sincerely,
Clarence

Southern Philippines

home
tropical climate   long coastline   numerous
  lakes & rivers
ideal for fishing   abacá
    farmers grew this crop for centuries
before Spanish
    & American colonists
        Filipino culture today:
a blend of Eastern   Western   & local
  traditions   Catholic celebration
Your connection to this region
is most likely through ancestors
linked to the Visayas & Mindanao
48%

Kimchi

Nothing gives me more hope
than spicy cabbage

with a bowl of steaming
wheat noodles in front of me,
I can finally be —

my Filipina mother didn't eat
ramen growing up, or like
kimchi, but my picture of Asia
was painted in America —

as an American, I can choose
from curated Eastern symbols —
Ghibli, kung fu, & K-pop —
I learn from the weeaboos
& down-low fetishists —

I'm the most Filipinx version
of myself with white friends
in a Japanese-style ramen shop —
Filipin*x*, not Filipin*o*,
not because of my non-binary
identity but because *x* marks me
as Anglo, barely yellow —

& the truth — I don't become
anything by eating kimchi,
no metamorphosis,
my face still a question —

China

List of Illustrations

Some figures (2, 3, & 6)
have been redacted from this catalog
due to copyright constraints.
The gallery apologizes in advance
for the inconvenience. We appreciate
your patronage & hope to see you
at our next event.

Figure 1. Unidentified artist, *Canton System*, ca. 1757–1842, loose leaf jasmine tea, silver coins, opium, & flotsam (polychromed) splattered against canvas (salted & sanded), 16 x 20 in. (40.6 x 50.8 cm.). National Museum of Anthropology / Ethnology Collection, City of Manila. (public domain; photograph provided by an unnamed Chinese donor)

//

[Redacted]

\\

[Redacted]

//

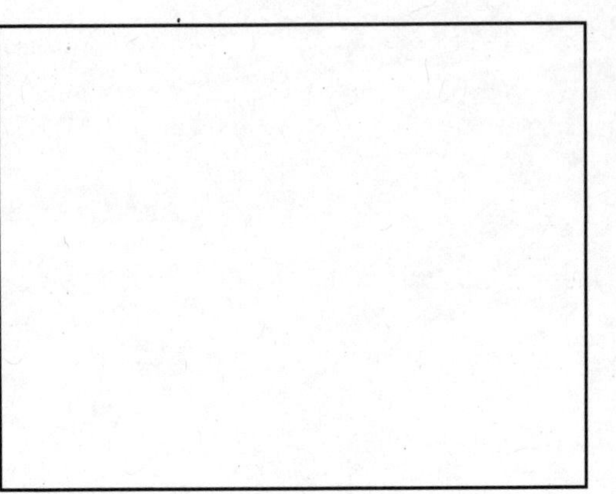

Figure 4. Sarah Dela Torre, *Catholic Girl*, ca. 1981–1985, cerulean skirt embroidered with schoo logo (frayed), crumpled handwritten letter dipped in perfume, packet of otap, & internship application (smudged & incomplete glued onto a light-damaged poster of Ton Selleck, 30 x 40 in. (76.2 x 101.6 cm.). Privat collection, City of Talisay. (artwork & photograph © The Dela Torre Family Trust)

\\

Figure 5. Richard Putney, *Military Triptych* (detail), ca. 1957–1965, half-empty carton of Lucky Strike cigarettes, battered copy of *The Art of War* by Sun Tzu, mail-order bride catalog (annotated), & sepia photo of a smiling woman (stained with an adhesive substance) rendered on wood with a mixture of egg tempera & liquid myrrh, 36 x 48 in. (91.4 x 121.9 cm.). Cherry Hill Farmhouse, Falls Church. (artwork & photograph © Sara Putney)

//

[Redacted]

\\

Figure 7. Unidentified artist (possibly East or Southeast Asian), *Living Ghost*, early 21st century, faded leather jewelry box with compartments containing green tea bags (generic), Poison eau de toilette by Dior, Marlboro cigarette butts, & a small sticker of a brown-skinned male figure with hole-punched eyes, 16 x 10 x 9.5 in. (40.6 x 25.4 x 24.1 cm.). Nevada Historical Society / Trails West Collection, Reno. (artwork & photograph copyright unknown)

Southern China

from the Yunnan & Sichuan
in the west   to Shanghai & Taiwan
in the east   geographically diverse
ancient civilizations began
cultivating tea & silk here
over 4,000 years ago   in time,
China became a center
for international trade   today the region
is famed for food —
delicate fare —
the beauty of its coastline
& mountains   & bustling, rising cities
like Guangzhou, Shenzhen, & Kunming
Your ethnicity estimate is 3%

Latex

Son, your great-great-
grandmother grew poppies
in South China.   *Respectable*,
the rhythm of your voice says.
I imagine the synapses
in your brain: bulbs oozing
yellow milk & the eyes of scorers
                    twinkling with success.

Son, it's hard work — multiple cuts
                    to bleed one teardrop.

        You ask: Was my great-great-
        grandma the harvester
        or the farm owner?
        I must come from a long line
        of strong Asian women.

Son, I want to tell you this is a reverie,
my mother's favorite origin story.
  But I can't —
                  there's no truth to share.

Siopao

Braised, not grilled —
how my bones will be cooked
upon death.   I'm a combo
covered in tattoos
   & chicken skin, the result
of moist volcanic lava
                    dipped
           in Great Basin salt.
Before my birth, there were sea
-ways connecting Cebu
            to Guangzhou.
  How do you think
 my mom was born?
Sometimes I wish I could lick   off
   the latex of Ma's memories
    to get to the tsismis.
Rumors: the only currency
  I share with family.
That   & our love
           of pork buns
     whorled like the whirlpool
   of my self-destructing body.
 All I can hope for is a good boiling
 to infuse my corpse
              with spice.
I come prepared for my ancestors,
  whose bellies
  will show me truth.

Colonization

Mestizo = Spanish + Indigenous (historical),
general term for mixed ancestry (contemporary) 500 years ago:
New Spain = Iberian Peninsula, northern South America,
American Southwest, Philippines, Guam, et al.
/
Tenochtitlan's fall, the beginning of expansion —
consider Manila, a wealthy entrepôt,
galleons & galleons & galleons,
Japanese & Chinese immigrants, Sangleys in the Parián,
ivory sculptures of the Infant Jesus, Virgin Mary bends light
like porcelain, *can you see the elephant's blood in the striations,*
crucifixion
\
mixing in the workshops,
Sino-Filipino babies, *who created the statuary,*
it resembles "China": arched eyebrows, rounded faces,
the art-historical record declares, the one primary source is evidence,
the native Filipinos thus a palimpsest
/ / my body not here, I try on breeches but have no bones,
no silver, no history \ \
the colonial event is a typhoon,
a flash of red —
I know about the Intramuros, the Pasig filth,
bathe me in sewage to anoint this tan skin:
I see towers
across time, an empire rising & falling,
I'm the aftermath (mestizaje),
a little Guangzhou on my fingers,
a lot of Cebu deep inside my scars, blink once
for the Viceroyalty, blink twice
for a temporal collapse —
the event is ongoing

Self-Orientalization

During the late Meiji period,
Japan publicized its hybrid West–
East period rooms filled with Japanese
art objects, an eclectic mix, to signal
"tradition," while the emperor visited
various residences (wearing shoes)
to bestow global imperial power
on the burgeoning nation-state.
In this way, the country is said
to have self-orientalized its artwork,
a show of ambivalence, an archipelago
caught in the growing pains of a rapidly
expanding globe — *we're here, we're*
powerful, too. I think this narrative
is mine, as if my body were historicized
into an era of 20th-century capitalism
& nationalism, my mycorrhizal DNA
invading every ocean. This must be why
I dreamed of Guangzhou yesterday,
my great-grandma's kiss resting
on my forehead, sweat transforming
my face into a facsimile of the future:
untraceable dirt. Where have I been
but a reflection off a colonizer's gun,
the opium burning in a bootstrapper's
pipe? Any connection to my past
can be found in Said's writing, an *I*
attempting to insert itself into a story
1,000 times lost via signification,
Derrida-style. Imagination is all I have
when history gives me nothing. Percent
this, percent that, but my blood burns
for a vigil full of ghosts. I want to know

who I am, but I only find my father's
grave. Am I already dead? Researching
Chinese culture, a piece of puto
in my mouth, I arrive at the valet lot
of nowhere. I'm forever gutom. Yes,
I breathe, I eat. & yes, my soul is right:
I'll never repay my debt of bones.

Interview with My Great-Grandmother

Diin ka natawo in South China?

[Ad-lib question about childhood?]

~~Why did you pursue a career in opium farming?~~
~~Why did you start working on an opium farm?~~
How old were you when you started working on the farm?

When did you move to the Philippines?

What was it like raising your daughter in Cebu?

Did you know your granddaughter lives in America?

Namatay ka?

~~Are you real?~~
Have you been inside me?

A Brief History of Jade

I finger my earrings & think motherland
where is it inside a boi-body
I shove tapers into my fistulas & hope & hope I may touch
the Maritime Jade Road
the salt of my mother's vessel her prehistoric sea changes
all the ghost bodies
on an inherited tongue is this loving myself I give Ma a bell jar
full of bones & tell her I've discovered our secrets
if you crush an animal's skeleton & drink the dust
you'll hear the miners clink nephrite swirls in our kidneys
I scratch my lower back raw
to find a nugget am I Asian enough am I Asian enough
I lick the blood off my fingertips (eureka)
I ask Ma for another pair of earrings & she nods in conspiracy
tells me she's proud caresses the jewels along the seaways
of my ears *imperial* I whisper every century of dust
remembered in holes every rise & fall kissing
my flesh she cups my cheek because she knows *do you hear it*
I ask & her eyes bloom & I taste the salt & she says
welcome

Multitude

At 24, I found Walt Whitman's infamous nude photo series. Almost scientific in their presentation, the images capture a decaying Whitman from various angles, ventral to dorsal. I traced the curvature of his extended left leg with my middle finger. I analyzed the shape of his pelvis. I imagined his conical beard tickling my neck. I was aroused.

I thought of Dad and choked on my spit. Twice the age of my preteen self, but I hadn't changed. Four years after his death, but I still wanted him.

Psychologists and social workers say it's normal for children to develop crushes on their parents. *Mommy, I want to marry you*, a 4- or 5-year-old boy declares. He pouts when Mommy tells him Daddy is already married to her. He demands that only Mommy tuck him in to bed. He envies Daddy — wishes he would disappear — so that he, alone, can cuddle with Mommy.

Adorable, some might call this behavior. *Part of growing up*, others might say. Friends, too, have shared such rites of passage with me, assurance that I'm simply another collection of organs with a human face.

What I don't tell them is that I yearned to kiss my dad at 12, not 4. I fantasized about his shirtless torso at 13, not 5. We shared a bed together every night through middle school, Ma in a separate room, my nose millimeters away from the salty tapestry of his back. I was his perfect son, Ma his imperfect wife. At night I'd conjure Ma's face, tilted downward during every dinnertime conversation. *Am I a replacement?* I'd think.

We didn't have sex, but I secretly hoped.

During the mid-1800s, it was common for American men to hug, kiss, and sleep in the same bed. This behavior was associated with friendship, the strong platonic bond that inevitably developed between two men. Because sexuality wasn't categorized — the term *homosexual* wouldn't be used until the late nineteenth century — these acts avoided controversy and institutional repression.

Whitman, however, sought to create a literary world encoded with homoerotic romance and pleasure, entire topographies budding with male–male companionship. He interpellated his lovers as comrades, men who could unite under the aegis of his newly formed queer democracy. Within this community, there would be more than brotherly pats on the back and pecks on the cheek.

In "Song of Myself," for example, Whitman depicts an orgy of 28 comrades bathing in a river. An onlooker, presenting as a woman, joins the bacchanal, his/her hand sensuously gliding along their wet chests. Through the speaker's embodiment of this onlooker, shifting from male god to womanly specter, he/she can enjoy fingering these men's bodies, glittering with spray, while avoiding detection from the heteronormative gaze.

Eighty years before my dad was born, he entered the universe as this orgiastic ghost — he must have. Rummaging through my dad's estate, I found a picture of a shirtless blond man at the beach with a disarming smile. Splattered with homoerotic dust, the image was tucked between photos of Dad's wives and children. I thumbed the man's face and thought *comradeship.*

When I came out, my dad mentioned this man, the one he loved before doubling down on heterosexuality. *I got over it*, he said to dissuade me from my gay reality. I don't believe him. If I could dismantle time, I'd relocate Dad's birth to the nineties or early aughts. He'd be happy, and I wouldn't exist.

Having little information, I choose to fabulate his and my dad's history: 1961, Luzon. The airmen's favorite haunt. A glance down the bar. A coughed-out *hello.* Fingers brushing for half a second. An invitation for a nightcap. Laughing over spilled beer. A glance across the couch. Fingers brushing for a second and a half. A coughed-out *Richard, I don't know.* The gap closing. A kiss, tentative. A kiss, oceanic.

❦

Allen Ginsberg famously imagines falling in love with the gay founding father of American poetry in a California supermarket. *Where are we going?* he asks on their odyssey through refrigerated meats, Whitman's gray beard the compass for their aisle-two romance. Touching *Leaves of Grass*, Ginsberg simultaneously strokes Whitman's paunch and wrinkled thighs, opening a transtemporal door to the cottage that houses their chickenhawk life.

This poem was written in 1955: Ginsberg a fresh 29, my dad a couple of years out from enlisting as an airman. Like Ginsberg, my dad was a twink in his youth. Neither was a full-blooded man yet, both chasing the specter of maleness through role models whose sole accomplishment was making it past 40.

I relish my dad and Ginsberg as twinks. In this suspended time frame, I can love one and stomach the other. Here, I glimpse a reflection of myself: prey, always on the run, refusing to stop. But them? My dad became a predator the day he impregnated a Filipina girl, his first of three wives, outside Luzon's Clark Air Base; Ginsberg, when he realized he could pursue boys under the age of 18, joining NAMBLA. The two became men.

❦

I'm a meaning lost in a loop of pederastic signification. If I deconstruct my pedigree, homoeroticism shakes out of every orifice. My lifelong attraction to mature men was never a glitch but an eventuality. Whitman has always been inside me, chronology be damned.

During junior high, I often pictured my male teachers, 20 to 30 years older, in nothing but swim trunks. I fixated on the chest hair that escaped from the tops of their shirts; what was underneath? *Mere curiosity*, I deflected to friends when letting my fantasies slip.

During high school, I crushed on my calculus teacher, a forty-something bald man with the pinkest pouty lip. I aced my AP exam because I enjoyed looking at him. On my ACT's writing section, I excavated his tan body, calling him a *glittery performer*; the scorers assigned that portion of the test a 33 for my *imagination*.

During undergrad, I was electrified by my professor, in his early 40s, lecturing our class about literary criticism. Queer theory and gender studies dripped from his teeth like caramelized honey. I imagined all the clichés: cheeks in hands, beard against stubble, lips ablaze. When he asked my underage self out for a drink, I knew my academic history, my gaze, had been real.

When I see male celebrities grow older, only becoming more attractive, I recall Whitman's "Calamus" cluster of poems. I start to mentally outline his ribbed breast, each scar and wrinkle its own constellation. I swear I feel his scented herbage brush the tip of my tongue. *Like aged wine*, I'm told.

When I navigate to the *Daddy* section of gay porn sites, Whitman's visage appears to me through my webcam and silently whispers Dad's name. I cope via post-coital dysphoria, by which I mean I scrub myself clean and sit alone in the dark after masturbation and sex. In this feral state I'll bite if touched.

Today, I look in the mirror and encounter a blur, a palimpsest of other men's history. I try to mourn my sexuality, but I don't know how to miss what was never mine. I'm an animal licking an invisible wound.

Is this what Whitman meant when he wrote, *I am large, I contain multitudes*?

❦

One of the first memories I have of my dad is him slamming Ma's head into the gravel of our driveway. He took her to the hospital, said it was an accident, then ferried her back home, bandage-clad. Dad brought me to her room to say hello, but I wanted to go outside and play with him instead.

This is the day I learned to crave abuse. To fuck an older man is to be destroyed. Ten years younger, four decades rewound, and I'd be Ginsberg's type. We'd howl together on our makeshift bed of recycled blankets and mismatched throw pillows. He'd extract every ounce of jouissance from my bones — the prospect of immolation thrills me. My flesh obliterated, I'm able to hear the whistle of inheritance through rectal tears: *Daddy, I'm coming home.*

I predictably take after Whitman. In "Song of Myself," he equates sex to death through the putrefaction of the fleshed body, miraculous in its noxious odors. He deems armpit sweat superior to prayer, the bowels just as delicate as a man's heart. He builds a religion out of bodily sensations and asserts the holiness of his corporeal form. This is my gospel.

Leo Bersani similarly defines the rectum as a grave, a site where ecstasy and annihilation intersect. To receive anal pleasure is to be powerless. But powerlessness is precisely the value of sexuality, for it's through the disintegration and humiliation of the self that we detach ourselves from heteropatriarchal expectations of sex. We reinvent our bodies, our rapture.

This must be it: my destruction, my remaking.

❦

According to Sigmund Freud, I should want to kill my dad. If the paradigm were reversed, I'd wish for Ma's death. Neither option works. What category exists for children who desire to be the locus of their fathers' devastation?

I refused to grow up, so I became non-binary. As a not-man, I avoid replicating my dad's abuse. Instead of wielding violence, I transform it into cosmic energy. I'd rather be haunted than haunt. Let me be fucked by every Whitman if it means one less ruiner in this waste land. I won't evolve into a Ginsbergian pedophile.

That isn't the whole truth. I collapsed into the interstices of gender during playfights with my childhood friends. They always beat me hard; I could barely get a punch in. I'd cry to my mom and think *why*. At 6 years old, I chose surrender.

As Oedipus and Electra's illegitimate child, I was born without a definable shape. I'm a nothing attempting to materialize my dad's ghost. Consuming him, I might morph into his twink form as a junior airman: dazed smile, eyelashes doused in stardust. *This is who I was always meant to be*, I try to believe.

In other words, I submit to older men hoping I find my face: the visage of a renegade who can finally stop running. Stillness — I imagine it tastes of salt.

❦

I'm sorry, Ma. For him. For me.

❦

Reconsidering Whitman's river-bathing scene, Michael Moon argues that the omnipresent speaker of "Song of Myself" doesn't supplant the female observer but journeys alongside her, the two participating in the orgy simultaneously. The onlooker's femininity lubricates the speaker's passage toward the river without sacrificing her agency; thus, the two figures' descent into bacchanalia is a collaboration, not a rivalry.

If my dad entered the spiritual plane as this observer, so, too, did my mom. As a teenager, Ma watched reruns of *Magnum, P.I.* in her Cebu home and yearned for Tom Selleck's touch. Little did she know that less than a decade later, she'd marry an ex-military, 6-foot plus mustache wearer more than twice her age. She was his third wife: another Filipina, a different island.

Ma chose to advertise herself in the Asian Romance catalog distributed to American men, immigrating to California as a 24-year-old picture bride. She was an agent, my dad her collaborator. I think she and I have the same type.

Extending Moon's analysis, I interpret the onlooker and speaker's dual presence as an amalgamation: femininity within masculinity. In this way, the spectral 29th bather transcends gendered expectations and experiences the kaleidoscope of affective states available to men and women. Whitman's queer democracy saturates each comrade with possibility.

Here, I'm alive-and-not. I exit time and space as the bodiless orgy-goer, a capacity waiting to be reached. I glimpse Dad and Ma, my invisible vellus hairs buzzing at the sight of our overlapping shadows. I wonder if they see me. I wonder if three phantoms can be a multitude.

❦

At a nondescript dive bar, I observe a tall man across the room: his hair, salt-and-pepper; torso, curved like a hawk over an empty glass. He glances at me. I half-smile; he offers the other half.

I fabulate our story: A coughed-out *hello*. Fingers brushing for half a second. An invitation for a nightcap. Laughing over spilled beer. A glance across the couch. Fingers brushing for a second and a half. A coughed-out *Dani, I don't know*. The gap closing. A kiss, tentative.

The ocean swells in my mouth. Kyler, Stephen, Alan — they all buzz across my synapses. I don't know this man's name, but I've already added him to my inventory. I feel Ma in my chest.

We start to walk toward one another. I contemplate sweet flags dying at the edge of my future grave. In his eyes, I see my reflected face: *I'm coming home.*

America

Los pioneros

En este camino
los hemos matado a todos.
Las caléndulas respiran
la sangre de sus memorias.
Los fantasmas se queman
por el cielo —
los rumores por el cosmos.
¿Los oyes? Al nacer
las mentiras se infiltran
por el suelo de la verdad —
nosotros no lo creemos.
La atmósfera está infectada,
¿la ves? El pasado
no nos dice nada —

Capitol

My pores crave freedom as I dog-
paddle through Farragut Square
moisture. Is this bliss, or is it
drowning? I cross these streets
after years of want, need — I must
swim among alba-marla giants.
My olive body finally made it
to the foggy bottom of our country,
where merit is currency & I'm rich.
I, too, can absorb 8 a.m. vapor.
Except giants don't exist. This isn't
a pond. Nobody's swimming. Men
commute while I lose my merit
in the crosshairs of 17th & H.

Naked Heat

Fireworks barrel through me
as I lean against the cool wall
of my room. This nation's
independence ricochets off
towers & sidewalks, festers
within me as District swelter
trickles down my thighs.
Hordes of strangers leave
the Mall with memories
to relive alongside their spouse-
plus-2.5-children boxes
back home. My sweat tells me
no: Night-sky chemicals may
thrill us, but this country will
kill us. Vibrations rupture
my yellow belly & spill blood
on the carpet. My chromosomes
burn in protest.

Germanic Europe

dramatic landscape
from Dutch & German lowlands
along the North Sea
through forested uplands
people were united
by language & culture before Germany
became a country in 1871
Das Land der Dichter und Denker,
home to some of the oldest universities
in the world   a long tradition
of producing scientists, inventors, theologians,
artists, & composers
Your ethnicity estimate is 28%
but can range from 25–47%

Ars Party Foul

You walked in with a vodka
cream soda, a concoction
you gave me to sip.
What do you think?
as if you didn't expect me
to say it was *strange yet*
appealing, as if my thought
wasn't manufactured to be
a gear in your cerebral machinery.
Tell me, old man, that we're not

the same. Maybe then I could believe
I didn't also perform intelligence
over American Spirits & Pinot
Grigio — *have you heard*
of Thomas James? — that my inter-
jections of Dickinsonian history
weren't a blight on the group
discourse, as I imagine
you call it. A frisson
down my spine reminded me

we were never alike, not
in your Upstate New York
bourgeois carapace of a child-
hood, nor in your body — big
& white, a man's man — that will
never feel the sting of less than.
If I touch your arm, can you feel
my bite marks? My story is graded
by scar count & the tablespoons
of fairy dust I use to cauterize

my wounds. Brown twinkbois must
protect ourselves, our precious
flesh, devoured by your kind,
old man. In two decades I'll arrive
at your midlife juncture, where you
realized you deserved a spot
at my friends' table, & I'll thank
anything other than God
that it was never possible
for me to become you.

Nature in Technicolor

Look at us, undead at the end
of our trail. A not-boy in the wild,
you glittering with sun-spray.
Nevada is the most mountainous
state — long lost a rite. Last week
a teenage girl's corpse emerged
from the valley surrounding
our convergent boundary. I think
of us in her place, Shepard
& *Brokeback* our inheritance,
but the truth is it would be me,
alone, lips painted green,
gold-pierced nose hidden
under coyote sand. Can a body
howl away its decomposition?
Caught in celebratory sagebrush,
water bottles at our lips (the prize
for foolishness), I simply smile
at you. Muir & Roosevelt didn't
see me, or me with you, at the peak
of America's wilderness. I half-
expect to die every time I caress
a mountaintop. I want to believe
the desert wind is free, the mantle
beneath our feet some great
equalizer, but I only grow darker
while you turn red. We bleed
differently, centuries of dirt
between us.   If I disappear, love,
know it's your fault for kissing
peril.

Permafrost

—

I remember being marooned
up Donner Pass, my dad at the wheel,
his howls at us to stop the snow,
the only danger inside   a man
cannibalizing his imports: children
& wife.

—

On our way to Portland
my best friend & I spun out, doused
in moonlight, tiny ice flakes dancing
then dying on the windshield   what
was the forest thinking, would it let us
die inside it.

—

I almost died near Vail
three years ago, no chains, no lights,
I willed the blizzard to kill me,
wouldn't it be romantic   a body
returned to their mountain father
& never found.

—

& now: I don't want kids, but all
I can think is if I had a child I'd call them
Tundra, or Nevada, the past participle
of nevar   a chill that lingers, as in
how have I made it through Albuquerque,
as in lo imposible.

Asian Romance Guide to Marriage by Correspondence

[Undated]

Dear Leticia,

Thanks for the letter
& photo you seem nice —
unfortunately, it is clear
our interests differ I want
a young lady

Best wishes,
James

PS: I decided to return your
[face], give it to another man

American Pastoral

On a patch of infected soil,
the last alfalfa plant burns,
tells a story of lives never lived.
Humans haven't touched this dirt.

Alfalfa burns under a dead sky,
nobody to witness the blaze.
Humans haven't touched anything
in ages. Blister beetles die by firelight.

Nobody gazes upon blazed
dirt — once green, tales say.
Blister beetles continue to die,
fiery wind propels their memories:

tales of green fields, they were called
farms. Alfalfa was grown to feed
horses, their bodies propelled by wind.
Like humans, the horses died,

along with the farms, now the alfalfa.
People's greatest talent was poisoning
their flesh, all the horses. What's left
is fire, a patch of infected soil.

Turning Point

Southbound on 95, the first real
turn you make from Fallon
to Las Vegas happens in Beatty,
a place famous for its straight shot
to Death Valley National Park
& candy shop. I never stay long —
forever a destination in mind —
but I'm always thrilled to reach
the small bend outside town.
Leading up to this curve
is the tiniest of rivers, the Amargosa,
only recognizable by way of shrubs
& riparian trees. If you look closely,
you can see the slightest of dips,
almost gully-like in its infancy.
When the river ends & I'm
on the highway's fulcrum, my body

projects into the mid-aughts,
fourth grade, my family's
summer expedition. Ma drank
enough water to drown her organs.
(Don't ask me why we didn't stop
in town.) Dad swerved onto sand
& we sprang out, van doors left
open, our roles already assigned.
Past a low fence my mom squatted
on the baby gully & pissed,
male bodies a wall around her.
Maybe it was pre–Independence Day
sentiment, but I felt American then.
Every family road trip has its
pee-in-the-water-bottle scare. Yes,
even those with yellow mothers,
yellow children.

Mixed

Cryogenesis

This one's for the kids
iced in time, trapped
in a psychedelic journey
through cerebra, the herbs
of their lives wafting through
stale air like cigarette smoke
feeding collapsible lungs;
their thermometers count down
to absolute zero — doomsday —
mercury flowing through frosted
glass, bodies encapsulated
in a chamber labeled *Reckoning*;
their hearts are locked,
beating silenced by lies told
to our children, valves made
inoperable by formaldehyde
chilled to preserve a dead
US

The Price of Olives

I'm the most beautiful person
I know. I'm an ancient Greek deity
by 21st-century postcolonial norms.
Did you know racial mixing
was illegal in America until 1967?
During *Loving v. Virginia*, my mom
was born across the Pacific —
it must have been cosmic. 29 years
& several wars later, my Visayan
aunties were pleased to welcome
ripe olive flesh into their tower:
We did it. No sun necessary
to darken my skin, no melanoma
price tag, but my chest still bleeds
Euro hegemony in the acne scars
beside my nipples, the tiny hairs
along my sternum. With Ma's color
& Dad's texture, I'm the poster
child for colorism across a group
of islands I only know by hearing
someone else's story. I want
to touch the history in my bones,
but all I feel is skin, beauty,
the American Dream. *We did it.*

Poem with Fake Resolution

Every mother of color has told me,
Yes, you're exactly what I've
wanted, as if a palimpsest
were the answer to a country

on the precipice of collapse.
My skin is a June bug
caught in some fool's hair,
you know the one, the person

who can't separate nature
from the dirt beneath their feet.
I nod & smile, a child raised right
by a mom like all the rest:

a teenage major in mixology.
I want to blame pop-culture
white boys with beautiful hair.
They're all a lie. Truth

doesn't scan postcolonial
QR codes. The future was
always kids' stuff, some dash
of cinnamon swirl to let would-

be mothers taste hope. I'd never
respond, *I'm not your blueprint*
to DIY, a detour in cake mixing.
Because I get it. Easier to scam

finality for a racialized world
than accept the nothing that will
inevitably materialize. I prefer
a spoonful of worms to fall

from acquaintances' mouths.
Predictable. *I'm lucky*, I reply.
I'm a global citizen.

Gathering Wood, 1998

Our ebony wheelbarrow,
his breath at my back,
logs of cedar? fir?
at my feet, little hands
suspended midair —
roller-coaster instincts.
Our forage was equal parts
survival & play,
he wanted me to have
adventure like he did,
younger, countries away.
I wanted love,
maybe more, I was stricken
by his gray mane
& mustache. Since then,
every chest under my tongue
has been a homecoming.
Daddy, I'm here,
can't you see me? I want
the roller coaster back,
my back against
your breath, we need wood
for our fire, Dad. I'm frost-
bitten without you.
I must re-create,
give me beards & musk —
musk, the not-enough
of men's flesh,
always older, never
the same gray luster.

Footnotes to Marriage by Correspondence

HER LETTERS

Almost all Filipinas think they are
unattractive, ordinary, shy ladies from poor
families   their culture expects them to be
simple, innocent virgins   is she lying
to you?   yes, & she knows it   courtship
by mail requires specific, creative questions,
but the rewards are sweet like [mangoes]
Warning Signs: you must guard
against the deceitful, "gold-digger" types
who would marry the first man to provide
a visa & plane ticket to America   gold-
diggers have been coached or have learned
their tactics through prostitution
Beware of the following: she says
she loves you in the first or second letter,
you discover that she smokes or drinks,
she sends lewd, revealing photos of herself,
or she talks about her desire for the good life
Exercise caution with these types:
high school dropouts, ladies from wealth,
hostesses, actresses, dancers   & attorneys
Most Filipinas you will be writing
cherish virginity, especially the young
teenagers   a few liberated ladies have
strayed from this tradition   we strongly
recommend that you proceed cautiously
with these [feminists]

Pauli Exclusion

I may not be a physicist,
but I know an atom's
electrons spin opposite: one half
positive, one half negative.
What this means is
even at matter's most basic,
we're unbalanced. Biologists claim
we're bilateral, like planaria cut
in two, though it's all a ruse:
dimorphic logic for a superficial
answer to similarity & difference.
No, our (a)symmetry isn't
                                        split into re-
cursive flatworms or clams or
any class of invertebrates,
our matter isn't the hemolymph
of beetles or grasshoppers or
praying mantises that wave hello
from my backdoor gable.
What if I said everything
                                        was chaos
composed of subatomic particles,
the smallest gyrations counter-
counter-clockwise, halfway left,
halfway right? No need to believe me
to understand the truth: What truth?
I'm not the first to say life
is a perception of reality. Our bodies
exist because we make them.
Scientists are simply masters
of justifying their observations
through repetition — but all I know,
                                                lies.

Anti-mimetic Body

A sculptural imitation:

When I'm attracted to masculinity,
I can't separate the urge to fuck
& to become. Riding denim
is how I evolve into myself,
a high most never reach.

When I'm drawn to femininity,
laws of nature disappear to align
my flat chest with spiked roses,
an emulsion defyingly miscible,
blue & pink —

no, I'm yellow & more yellow,
infinity in the cosmos of my marrow,
a solute always dissolving. Spare me
from coupledom, that severance
which fails to mimic my elastic body.

First Date

To all the men I've ever loved

What if I told you I was a cannibal,
born right next to Donner Pass?
I've lived along this path since 1846,

when many of my ancestors perished.
My body emerged 150 years later
as a parasitic fungus in the shape

of a human. Biologists call my birth
parthenogenesis, like the Komodo
dragon, a something sprouting

from nothing: me, the unfertilized egg
of fossilized nails & teeth. Sarap.
All this I'd say on our first date,

a chunk of rare bison steak gracing
the tip of my knife. Because I don't
care about my mental well-being,

I opt for truth:
                    a not-boy transcribed
from DNA stuck in a centuries-long

imperial takeover, skin glowing
like the shine in a eugenicist's eyes.
I'm his experiment gone right to keep

Asia's skin-whitening market deep
in the black. I exist because a white
man willed it. I tell you I wake up

every morning ashamed to be what
two people across the globe wanted:
mestizo, a word vouchsafed to me

by generations of Spanish rapists
& a father who cut out my second
tongue to fit my mouth around

his legacy of Mid-Atlantic marlstone.
I'm the ultimate possibility, by which
I mean I wither beside my family tree,

hoping an apple or a coconut cracks
my skull to make me real. Can you
help me understand why I'm alive?

No, I get it, you prefer the creature
risen from mountainside detritus, birth
strange but definable, origin manifest

in your US history textbook: *Hi again,*
I'm Georgie, named after my great-
great-grandpa who braved the Sierra

before dying in a blizzard.

Mosquitoes

Swarm my olive visage,
buzz from ear to ear,
dance to the thump-thump
behind veiny temples. Carry
my vascularity into the time warp,
twirl me out of reality.

I descend this staircase rife
with blood loss, forget about physicality,
become a forager of the in-between.
Listen — parasite warbles,
soul-suckers of the void:
One, two, wingbeat. One, two, wingbeat.

In this upside-down,
I float above grandfather clocks,
white picket fences, baby-faced humanity:
no future for me.
Bugs consume the carcass of materiality,
vomit nothingness over my brown carapace.

This work of art is

an indictment. Your white-
flight prayers book-
ended with exclamation
marks & empty anecdotes
won't reach me. I don't want
your mouth full of flies.
I want the parcel of valley
stolen by your ancestors,
your hundreds of years
of money bags & livestock,
your muscle ripped between
my teeth. Did I stutter?
Your statements of diversity
& inclusion don't sate
my vampiric hunger:
I'd rather you didn't atrophy
good meat in CEO & director
roles assigned at birth.
My legacy? A paternal
Southeast Asian fetish
& yearning for an archipelago
denied to me at conception.
Skip the consolation,
just give me your body.
I can sell the colorless
skin for a modest price
so long as there's no
cancer.

Notes

Unless bracketed, the words in each installment of "Asian Romance Guide to Marriage by Correspondence" and "Footnotes to Marriage by Correspondence" are taken from sample letters and how-to sections, respectively, included in Michael and Chantal Donahue's *Asian Romance Guide to Marriage by Correspondence* (1989). Some phrasing has been reformulated.

The words in "Southern Philippines," "Southern China," and "Germanic Europe" come from descriptions included within each poem's respective category of AncestryDNA®. Some text formatting has been applied.

Acknowledgments

Thank you to the following magazines, journals, and anthologies for first publishing these pieces, most in earlier forms:

Azahares: "Los pioneros"
Barrelhouse: "Balikbayan," "Latex," "List of Illustrations"
beestung: "American Pastoral," "Heritage"
Bennington Review: "Footnotes to Marriage by Correspondence"
Brushfire Literature & Arts: "Picasso Bleeds"
Burning Jade Literary & Arts Magazine: "Dear Darren Criss"
Cream City Review: "Kumusta"
Dovecote Magazine: "Pauli Exclusion"
The Emerson Review: "Dela Torre," "The Price of Olives"
Faultline Journal of Arts and Letters: "Colonization"
Figure 1: "Coordinates for My Dad's Ashes"
FOLIO: "Capitol"
Glassworks Magazine: "Turning Point"
Grist: A Journal of the Literary Arts: "Germanic Europe," "Southern China," "Southern Philippines" (all as part of the poem sequence "Triple Helix")
Gulf Stream Magazine: "Ars Party Foul"
Hairstreak Butterfly Review: "Asian Romance Guide to Marriage by Correspondence"
Hayden's Ferry Review, The Dock: "Siopao"
Kissing Dynamite, Lift Every Voice: "Naked Heat"
Lucky Jefferson: "A Brief History of Jade"
Okay Donkey Magazine: "Dear Andrew Cunanan"
Palette Poetry: "First Date"
Pedestal Magazine: "Permafrost"
Prismatica Magazine: "Mosquitoes"
Puerto del Sol: "Nature in Technicolor," "Poem with Fake Resolution"

Quarter After Eight: "Self-Orientalization"
Quarterly West: "Multitude" (as "Walt Whitman Is the Reason I Want to Fuck My Dad")
The Racket: "Gathering Wood, 1998," "This work of art is"
Rappahannock Review: "Halo-halo"
Rigorous: "Cryogenesis"
Rust + Moth: "Kimchi"
Tinderbox Poetry Journal: "Killing Field"
Tolsun Books, *The Book of Life After Death*: "Interview with My Great-Grandmother" (as "Ten-Item Questionnaire for My Great-Grandmother")
Wend: "Anti-mimetic Body" (as "What the Ocean Taught Me")

Thank you to Sundress Publications, especially my editor, Kathleen Gullion, for publishing several of the poems in this collection in the chapbook *Dela Torre*: "Coordinates for My Dad's Ashes," "Cryogenesis," "Dela Torre," "Gathering Wood, 1998," "Halo-halo," "Heritage," "Killing Field," "Kimchi," "Los pioneros," "Naked Heat," "Otap," "Pauli Exclusion," "Picasso Bleeds," "The Price of Olives," "This work of art is," "Turning Point."

Thank you to Bullshit Press for publishing "Kumusta" and "Multitude" in the chapbook *Swallow Whole*.

Thank you to the amazing team at Baobab Press — Christine Kelly, Danilo John Thomas, and Laura Wetherington — for not only making this book a reality but also helping me shape it into what it is today. Y'all rock.

Thank you to graduate professors Sarah Beth Childers, Janine Joseph, Lisa Lewis, and Laura Minor for providing incredibly helpful comments and suggestions on many of the poems in this collection. This book wouldn't exist without your support.

Thank you to my colleagues at Oklahoma State University, especially Aly Allen, Allyn Bernkopf, Roseanna Alice Boswell, Brianne Grothe,

Whitney Koo, April Lim, Jenn Lobaugh Conner, Remi Recchia, Saga Savage, and Caleigh Shaw. Your feedback on earlier iterations of these poems has enabled them to become what they are today. Also, a special shout-out to A. Poythress for being my non-binary partner in crime at OSU.

And Breanna Inga: I can never thank you enough.

Dani Putney is a queer, non-binary, mixed-race Filipinx, and neurodivergent writer originally from Sacramento, California. Their debut full-length collection, *Salamat sa Intersectionality* (Okay Donkey Press, 2021), was a finalist for the 2022 Lambda Literary Award in Transgender Poetry. They are also the author of the poetry chapbook *Dela Torre* (Sundress Publications, 2022) and the creative nonfiction chapbook *Swallow Whole* (Bullshit Press, 2024). Their poetry appears in outlets such as *Bennington Review*, *Cream City Review*, *Grist*, *Hayden's Ferry Review*, and *Puerto del Sol*, among others, while their personal essays can be found in journals such as *Crab Creek Review*, *Glassworks Magazine*, and *Quarterly West*, among others. They received their PhD in English from Oklahoma State University and their MFA in Creative Writing from Mississippi University for Women. They live in Reno, Nevada.

Cormorant is an open-source serif family designed by Christian Thalmann. The design was inspired by the sixteenth-century types of Claude Garamond; however, in contrast to typical Garamond-inspired text faces, Cormorant was designed as a display face. The family is available in five distinct versions: *Cormorant* is the standard version, and *Cormorant Garamond* features larger counters that make it more suitable as a text face.